SOCC...

THE INTE... ...AL

LINE-UPS & ...TATISTICS

SERIES –

CHILE

1910-1970

STATISTICS
R.G. Hope-Smith

EDITOR
Michael Robinson

Price
£5.95

British Library Cataloguing in Publication Data
A catalogue record for this book is available from the British Library
ISBN 1-86223-027-7

Printed by Joshua Horgan Print Partnership, 246 Marston Road, Oxford, OX3 0EL

1: 27th May 1910
v ARGENTINA *Buenos Aires*
L. Gibson
C. Hormazábal
L. Barriga
A. Hoyl
H. Allen
P. González
A. Acuna
F. Simmons
C. Campbell
J. Hamilton
J. Davidson
Result 1-3 Simmons

2: 29th May 1910
v URUGUAY *Buenos Aires*
L. Gibson
J. MacWilliams
E. Ashe
C. Hormazábal
H. Allen
P. González
A. Acuna
F. Simmons
C. Campbell
J. Hamilton
J. Robson
Result 0-3

3: 5th June 1910
v ARGENTINA *Buenos Aires*
L. Gibson
J. MacWilliams
E. Ashe
C. Hormazábal
H. Allen
P. González
J. Robson
C. Campbell
H. Sturgess
J. Hamilton
J. Davidson
Result 1-5 Campbell

4: 21st September 1913
v ARGENTINA *Valparaiso*
R. Lester
O. Ernst
E. Cardenas
C. González
H. Dean
A. Elgueta
M. Geldes
P. Brito
A. Skewes
E. Teuche
J. Johnston
Result 0-2

5: 2nd July 1916
v URUGUAY (SAC) *Buenos Aires*
M. Guerrero
E. Cardenas
M. Wittke
E. Abello
E. Teuche
R. Unzaga
M. Geldes
R. Moreno
E. Gutiérrez
E. Fuentes
H. Salazar
Result 0-4

6: 6th July 1916
v ARGENTINA (SAC)
Buenos Aires
M. Guerrero
E. Cardenas
M. Wittke
E. Abello
E. Teuche
R. Unzaga
M. Geldes
A. France
E. Gutiérrez
E. Fuentes
T. Baez
Result 1-6 Baez

7: 8th July 1916
v BRAZIL (SAC) *Buenos Aires*
M. Guerrero
E. Cardenas
M. Wittke
E. Abello
E. Teuche
R. Unzaga
M. Geldes
A. France
E. Gutiérrez
H. Salazar
T. Baez
Result 1-1 Salazar

8: 12th July 1916
v ARGENTINA *Buenòs Aires*
J. Paredas
E. Cardenas
M. Wittke
E. Abello
E. González
R. Unzaga
E. Fuentes
E. Teuche
N. Vásquez
A. France
T. Baez
Result 0-1

9: 14th July 1916
v URUGUAY *Montevideo*
M. Guerrero
E. Cardenas
M. Wittke
E. Abello
E. González
R. Unzaga
E. Fuentes
E. Teuche
M. Vásquez
A. France
T. Baez
Result 1-4 France

10: 30th September 1917
v URUGUAY (SAC) *Montevideo*
M. Guerrero
F. Gatica
E. Cardenas
L.A. García
H. Baeza
G. Cisternas
M. Geldes
R. Rojas
B. Munoz
L. Encina
J. Paredes
Result 0-4

11: 6th October 1917
v ARGENTINA (SAC) *Montevideo*
M. Guerrero
F. Gatica
E. Cardenas
N. Guevara
L.A. García
J. Alvarado
H. Bolados
R. Rojas
B. Munoz
H. Munoz
J. Paredes
Result 0-1

12: 12th October 1917
v BRAZIL (SAC) *Montevideo*
M. Guerrero
E. Cardenas
F. Gatica
L.A. García
N. Guevara
J. Alvarado
H. Bolados
R. Rojas
B. Munoz
H. Munoz
J. Paredes
Result 0-5

13: 22nd October 1917
v ARGENTINA *Buenos Aires*
L.A. García
F. Gatica
R. Rojas
H. Baeza
G. Cisternas
J. Alvarado
M. Geldes
L. Encina
B. Munoz
H. Munoz
J. Paredes
Result 1-1 B. Munoz

14: 11th May 1919
v BRAZIL (SAC) *Rio de Janeiro*
M. Guerrero
P. Gatica
U. Poirer
O. González
H. Baeza
T. Baez
E. Fuentes
Au. Domínguez
A. France
H. Munoz
V. Varas
Result 0-6

15: 17th May 1919
v URUGUAY (SAC) *Rio de Janeiro*
M. Guerrero
P. Gatica
U. Poirer
O. González
H. Baeza
T. Baez
C. Del Rio
Au. Domínguez
A. France
E. Fuentes
V. Varas
Result 0-2

16: 22nd May 1919
v ARGENTINA (SAC)
Rio de Janeiro
M. Guerrero
P. Gatica
U. Poirer
O. González
H. Baeza
A. France
E. Fuentes
Au. Domínguez
H. Munoz
G. Frez
C. Del Rio
Result 1-4 France

17: 11th September 1920
v BRAZIL (SAC) *Valparaíso*
M. Guerrero
P. Vergara
U. Poirer
H. Elgueta
V. Toro
R. Unzaga
V. Varas
Au. Domínguez
Blas Parra
A. France
H. Munoz
Result 0-1

18: 20th September 1920
v ARGENTINA (SAC) *Valparaíso*
M. Guerrero
P. Vergara
U. Poirer
H. Elgueta
V. Toro
R. Unzaga
V. Varas
Au. Domínguez
H. Bolados
A. France
H. Munoz
Result 1-1 Bolados

19: 26th September 1920
v URUGUAY (SAC) *Valparaíso*
M. Guerrero
P. Vergara
U. Poirer
H. Elgueta
V. Toro
R. Unzaga
V. Varas
Au. Domínguez
H. Bolados
A. France
H. Munoz
Result 1-2 Au. Domínguez

20: 25th September 1921
v ARGENTINA *Valparaíso*
M. Guerrero
P. Vergara
U. Poirer
H. Elgueta
G. Saavedra
R. Unzaga
V. Varas
Au. Domínguez
H. Bolados
E. Fuentes
H. Munoz
Result 1-4 Saavedra

21: 17th September 1922
v BRAZIL (SAC) *Rio de Janeiro*
A. Bernal
P. Vergara
U. Poirer
H. Elgueta
R. Catalán
O. González
E. Abello
Au. Domínguez
M. Bravo
L. Encina
V. Varas
Result 1-1 Bravo

22: 23rd September 1922
v URUGUAY (SAC) *Rio de Janeiro*
P. Balbontín
P. Vergara
U. Poirer
H. Elgueta
R. Catalán
O. González
E. Abello
Au. Domínguez
M. Bravo
L. Encina
V. Varas
Result 0-2

23: 28th September 1922
v ARGENTINA (SAC)
Rio de Janeiro
P. Balbontín
P. Vergara
U. Poirer
H. Elgueta
R. Catalán
O. González
E. Abello
Au. Domínguez
M. Bravo
M. Ramirez
V. Varas
Result 0-4

24: 5th October 1922
v PARAGUAY (SAC)
Rio de Janeiro
A. Bernal
P. Zavala
U. Poirer
H. Elgueta
R. Catalán
O. González
E. Abello
Au. Domínguez
M. Ramirez
L. Encina
V. Varas
Result 0-3

25: 22nd October 1922
v ARGENTINA *Buenos Aires*
A. Bernal
P. Vergara
U. Poirer
H. Elgueta
V. Toro
R. Unzaga
E. Abello
Au. Domínguez
M. Bravo
M. Ramirez
V. Varas
Result 0-1

26: 25th November 1923
v URUGUAY *Montevideo*
A. Bernal
E. Cardenas
U. Poirer
H. Elgueta
V. Toro
O. González
E. Fuentes
Au. Domínguez
M. Ramirez
E. Leiva
J. Olguín
Result 1-2 Leiva

27: 3rd December 1923
v ARGENTINA *Buenos Aires*
A. Bernal
P. Vergara
U. Poirer
H. Elgueta
V. Toro
O. González
E. Fuentes
Au. Domínguez
E. Leiva
L. Encina
J. Olguín
Result 0-6

28: 19th October 1924
v URUGUAY (SAC) *Montevideo*
M. Ramirez
O. Ernst
P. Hamablet
E. Arellano
V. Toro
V. Morales
L. Abarzua
G. Reyes
Au. Domínguez
P. Molina
J. Olguín
Result 0-5

29: 25th October 1924
v ARGENTINA (SAC) *Montevideo*
C. Robles
O. Ernst
P. Hamablet
E. Arellano
V. Toro
V. Morales
L. Abarzua
G. Reyes
Au. Domínguez
P. Molina
J. Olguín
Result 0-2

30: 1st November 1924
v PARAGUAY (SAC) *Montevideo*
M. Ramirez
O. Ernst
P. Hamablet
E. Arellano
V. Toro
V. Morales
L. Abarzua
D. Arellano
Au. Domínguez
G. Reyes
J. Olguín
Result 1-3 D. Arellano

31: 12th October 1926
v BOLIVIA (SAC) *Santiago*
G. Hill
C. Velloso
U. Poirer
E. Sánchez
G. Saavedra
O. González
L.A. García
G. Subiabre
M. Ramirez
D. Arellano
R. Moreno

Result 7-1 Subiabre, Ramirez, Arellano 4, Moreno

32: 17th October 1926
v URUGUAY (SAC) *Santiago*
R. Cortés
C. Velloso
U. Poirer
E. Sánchez
G. Saavedra
O. González
L.A. García
G. Subiabre
R. Moreno
D. Arellano
J. Olguín

Result 1-3 Subiabre

33: 31st October 1926
v ARGENTINA (SAC) *Santiago*
R. Cortés
C. Velloso
U. Poirer
V. Toro
G. Saavedra
O. González
R. Moreno
G. Subiabre
M. Ramirez
D. Arellano
J. Olguín

Result 1-1 Saavedra

34: 3rd November 1926
v PARAGUAY (SAC) *Santiago*
R. Cortés
R. Figueroa
U. Poirer
V. Morales
G. Saavedra
O. González
R. Moreno
G. Subiabre
M. Ramirez
D. Arellano
J. Olguín

Result 5-1 Subiabre 3, Arellano 2

35: 10th December 1927
v URUGUAY *Vina del Mar*
R. Cortés
M. Chaparro
U. Poirer
V. Morales
G. Saavedra
H. Elgueta
R. Moreno
G. Subiabre
M. Bravo
R. Alfaro
J. Olguín

Result 2-3 Alfaro 2

36: 27th May 1928
v PORTUGAL (OG) *Amsterdam*
J. Ibacache
M. Chaparro
V. Morales
A. Torres
G. Saavedra
R.Alfaro
F. Contreras
C. Schenerberger
G. Subiabre
L. Carbonell
J. Olguín

Result 2-4 Subiabre, Carbonell

37: 4th June 1928
v MEXICO (OG) *Arnhem*
J. Ibacache
G. Riveros
M. Chaparro
A. Torres
G. Saavedra
V. Morales
C. Schenerberger
G. Subiabre
R. Alfaro
R. Arías
J. Olguín
Result 3-1 Subiabre 3

38: 8th June 1928
v HOLLAND (OG) *Rotterdam*
J. Ibacache
M. Chaparro
J. Linford
A. Torres
G. Riveros
V. Morales
R. Arías
G. Subiabre
M. Bravo
R. Alfaro
L. Carbonell
Result 2-2 Bravo, Alfaro

39: 16th July 1930
v MEXICO (WC) *Montevideo*
R. Cortés
V. Morales
U. Poirer
A. Torres
G. Saavedra
H. Elgueta
T. Ojeda
G. Subiabre
E. Villalobos
C. Vidal
C. Schenerberger
Result 3-0 Subiabre 2, Vidal

40: 19th July 1930
v FRANCE (WC) *Montevideo*
R. Cortés
M. Chaparro
V. Morales
A. Torres
G. Saavedra
C. Torres
T. Ojeda
G. Subiabre
E. Villalobos
C. Vidal
C. Schenerberger
Result 1-0 Subiabre

41: 22nd July 1930
v ARGENTINA (WC) *Montevideo*
R. Cortés
M. Chaparro
V. Morales
A. Torres
G. Saavedra
C. Torres
G. Arellano
G. Subiabre
E. Villalobos
C. Vidal
J. Aguilera
Result 1-3 Subiabre

42: 6th January 1935
v ARGENTINA (SAC) *Lima*
R. Cortés
R. Welch
A. Cortés
A. Gornali
G. Riveros
M. Araneda
M. Aviles
C. Vidal
A. Carmona (sub. E. Sorrel)
C. Giudice
P. Aranda
Result 1-4 Carmona

43: 18th January 1935
v URUGUAY (SAC) *Lima*
R. Cortés
R. Welch
A. Cortés
M. Araneda
G. Riveros
A. Gornali
C. Vidal
A. Carmona
J. Avendano
C. Giudice
P. Aranda
Result 1-2 Giudice

44: 26th January 1935
v PERU (SAC) *Lima*
R. Cortés
R. Welch
A. Cortés
M. Araneda
G. Riveros
A. Gornali
M. Aviles
C. Vidal
A. Carmona
C. Giudice
P. Aranda
Result 0-1

45: 30th December 1936
v ARGENTINA (SAC)
Buenos Aires
L. Cabrera
A. Cortés
J. Cordova
C. Montero
G. Riveros
C. Schenerberger
C. Torres
E. Corral
R. Toro
J. Avendano
T. Ojeda
Result 1-2 Toro

46: 3rd January 1937
v BRAZIL (SAC) *Buenos Aires*
L. Cabrera
A. Cortés
J. Cordova
C. Montero
G. Riveros
L. Ponce
C. Torres
M. Arancibia
R. Toro
J. Avendano
T. Ojeda (sub. M. Aviles)
Result 4-6 Riveros, Toro 2, Avendano

47: 10th January 1937
v URUGUAY (SAC) *Buenos Aires*
L. Cabrera
A. Cortés
J. Cordova
C. Montero
G. Riveros
L. Ponce
M. Aviles (sub. T. Ojeda)
J. Avendano
R. Toro
A. Carmona
C. Torres (sub M. Arancibia)
Result 3-0 Toro 2, Arancibia

48: 17th January 1937
v PARAGUAY (SAC) *Buenos Aires*
L. Cabrera
A. Cortés
J. Cordova
C. Montero
G. Riveros
L. Ponce
C. Torres
M. Arancibia (sub. A. Carmona)
R. Toro
J. Avendano
T. Ojeda
Result 2-3 Toro 2

49: 21st January 1937
v PERU (SAC) *Buenos Aires*
L. Cabrera
A. Cortés
J. Cordova
C. Montero
G. Riveros
L. Ponce
C. Torres
M. Arancibia (sub. A. Carmona)
R. Toro
J. Avendano (sub. M. Aviles)
T. Ojeda
Result 2-2 Torres, Carmona

50: 15th January 1939
v PARAGUAY (SAC) *Lima*
M. Simian
J. Roa
Jorge Cordova
C. Montero
G. Riveros
L. Ponce (sub. Julio Cordova)
E. Sorrel
R. Toro
Al. Domínguez
D. Carbajal
J. Avendano (sub. R. Luco)
Result 1-5 Sorrel

51: 22nd January 1939
v PERU (SAC) *Lima*
A. Lobos
A. Cortés
Jorge Cordova
C. Montero
M. Mediavilla
L. Ponce
E. Sorrel
G. Pizarro
R. Toro (sub. Al. Domínguez)
D. Carbajal
R. Munoz
Result 1-3 Al. Domínguez

52: 29th January 1939
v URUGUAY (SAC) *Lima*
A. Lobos (sub. M. Simian)
Jorge Cordova
A. Cortés
Julio Cordova
G. Riveros (sub. M. Mediavilla)
L. Ponce
E. Sorrel (sub R. Luco)
G. Pizarro
Al. Domínguez
J. Avendano
R. Munoz
Result 2-3 Luco, Munoz

53: 5th February 1939
v ECUADOR (SAC) *Lima*
M. Simian
Jorge Cordova
A. Cortés
Julio Cordova
G. Riveros
L. Ponce
E. Sorrel
G. Pizarro
R. Toro
J. Avendano
R. Luco
Result 4-1 Sorrel, Toro, Avendano 2

54: 26th February 1939
v PARAGUAY *Santiago*
M. Simian
Jorge Cordova
A. Cortés
Julio Cordova
G. Riveros
L. Ponce
E. Sorrel
G. Pizzaro
R. Toro
J. Avendano
R. Munoz
Result 2-4 Sorrel, Toro

55: 2nd March 1940
v ARGENTINA *Buenos Aires*
S. Livingstone
S. Salfate
A. Cordoba
S. Florez
M. Nocetti
L. Ponce
E. Sorrel
Al. Domínguez
H. Bolanos (sub. M. Cordoba)
M. Lira
R. Munoz
Result 1-4 Sorrel

56: 9th March 1940
v ARGENTINA *Buenos Aires*
S. Livingstone
S. Salfate (sub. J. Ellis)
A. Cordoba
S. Florez
M. Nocetti
L. Ponce (sub. J. Pastenes)
E. Sorrel
Al. Domínguez
H. Bolanos
G. Pizarro
R. Munoz
Result 2-3 Pizarro, Munoz

57: 5th January 1941
v ARGENTINA *Santiago*
S. Livingstone
H. Roa
S. Salfate
S. Florez
A. Castillo
J. Pastenes
E. Sorrel
S. Ramos (sub. P. Nortín)
R. Toro
J. Alonso
F. Riera (sub. R. Munoz)
Result 1-2 Alonso

58: 9th January 1941
v ARGENTINA *Santiago*
S. Livingstone
H. Roa
S. Salfate
J. Trejos
C. Pasache
S. Florez
F. Riera (sub. A. Balbuena)
J. Alonso
R. Toro
A. Contreras
E. Sorrel
Result 2-5 Balbuena, Sorrel

59: 2nd February 1941
v ECUADOR (SAC) *Santiago*
S. Livingstone
H. Roa
J. Ellis
M. Arancibia
A. Cabrera
J. Pastenes
E. Sorrel
D. Carbajal
R. Toro
A. Contreras
R. Pérez
Result 5-0 Sorrel 2, Toro, Contreras, Pérez

60: 9th February 1941
v PERU (SAC) *Santiago*
S. Livingstone
H. Roa
M. Vidal
S. Florez
A. Cabrera
J. Trejos
E. Sorrel
Al. Domínguez
R. Toro
L. Ruiz
R. Pérez
Result 1-0 Pérez

61: 16th February 1941
v URUGUAY (SAC) *Santiago*
S. Livingstone
H. Roa
M. Vidal (sub. A. Cortés)
S. Florez
A. Cabrera
J. Trejos
E. Sorrel
Al. Domínguez (sub. D. Carbajal)
R. Toro
L. Ruiz
D. Medina
Result 0-2

62: 4th March 1941
v ARGENTINA (SAC) *Santiago*
S. Livingstone
H. Roa
M. Vidal
S. Florez
A. Cabrera
J. Trejos (sub. J. Pastenes)
R. Munoz (sub. E. Sorrel)
D. Carbajal
R. Toro
A. Contreras
R. Pérez
Result 0-1

63: 10th January 1942
v URUGUAY (SAC) *Montevideo*
T. Ibanez (sub. H. Fernández)
S. Salfate
H. Roa (sub. M. Arancibia)
F. Las Heras
J. Pastenes
O. Medina
P. Armingol
A. Casanovas
Al. Domínguez
A. Contreras
G. Torres
Result 1-6 Contreras

64: 14th January 1942
v BRAZIL (SAC) *Montevideo*
H. Fernández
S. Salfate
H. Roa
F. Las Heras
J. Pastenes
O. Medina
P. Armingol
A. Casanovas
Al. Domínguez (sub. F. Barrera)
A. Contreras
G. Torres
Result 1-6 Al. Domínguez

65: 22nd January 1942
v PARAGUAY (SAC) *Montevideo*
S. Livingstone
S. Salfate
H. Roa
J. Pastenes
A. Cabrera
O. Medina
P. Armingol
F. Barrera
Al. Domínguez
A. Contreras (sub. M. Arancibia)
F. Riera (sub. A. Casanovas)
Result 0-2

66: 31st January 1942
v ARGENTINA (SAC) *Montevideo*
S. Livingstone
S. Salfate
H. Roa
J. Pastenes
A. Cabrera
O. Medina
P. Armingol
F. Barrera
Al. Domínguez
A. Contreras
F. Riera
Result 0-0 This match was abandoned after 43 minutes and was awarded to Argentina.

67: 5th February 1942
v ECUADOR (SAC) *Montevideo*
S. Livingstone
S. Salfate
H. Roa
J. Pastenes
A. Cabrera
O. Medina
P. Armingol
F. Barrera (sub. A. Casanovas)
Al. Domínguez
A. Contreras
F. Riera
Result 2-1 Armingol, Al. Domínguez

68: 7th February 1942
v PERU (SAC) *Montevideo*
S. Livingstone
S. Salfate
H. Roa
J. Pastenes
A. Cabrera
O. Medina
A. Casanovas (sub. F. Barrera)
Al. Domínguez
A. Contreras (sub. M. Arancibia)
F. Riera
P. Armingol
Result 0-0

69: 14th January 1945
v ECUADOR (SAC) *Santiago*
S. Livingstone
F. Barrera
H. Klein
F. Las Heras
F. Hormazábal
N. Ataglich
R. Pineiro
G. Clavero
J. Alcantara
A. Contreras (sub. A. Vera)
D. Medina
Result 6-3 Hormazábal, Clavero 2, Alcantara 2, Vera

70: 24th January 1945
v BOLIVIA (SAC) *Santiago*
S. Livingstone
F. Barrera
J. Vázquez
J. Pastenes
F. Las Heras
N. Ataglich (sub. M. Busquets)
R. Pineiro
G. Clavero
J. Alcantara
A. Vera (sub. A. Contreras)
D. Medina
Result 5-0 Clavero 2, Alcantara 2, Medina

71: 31st January 1945
v COLOMBIA (SAC) *Santiago*
S. Livingstone
F. Barrera
J. Vázquez (sub. H. Roa)
M. Busquets
J. Pastenes
F. Las Heras
R. Pineiro
G. Clavero
J. Alcantara
A. Contreras (sub. A. Cremaschi)
D. Medina
Result 2-0 Pineiro, Medina

72: 11th February 1945
v ARGENTINA (SAC) *Santiago*
S. Livingstone
F. Barrera
J. Vázquez
F. Las Heras
J. Pastenes
M. Busquets
R. Pineiro (sub. P. Armingol)
G. Clavero
F. Hormazábal
A. Vera (sub. C. Varela)
D. Medina (sub. A. Contreras)
Result 1-1 Medina

73: 18th February 1945
v URUGUAY (SAC) *Santiago*
S. Livingstone
F. Barrera
J. Vázquez
F. Las Heras
M. Busquets
J. Pastenes (sub. N. Ataglich)
R. Pineiro
G. Clavero
F. Hormazábal
A. Contreras (sub. A. Vera)
D. Medina (sub. M. Castro)
Result 1-0 Medina

74: 28th February 1945
v BRAZIL (SAC) *Santiago*
S. Livingstone
F. Barrera
J. Vázquez
F. Las Heras
M. Busquets
J. Pastenes
R. Pineiro
G. Clavero
F. Hormazábal (sub. N. Ataglich)
A. Vera
D. Medina
Result 0-1

75: 16th January 1946
v URUGUAY (SAC) *Buenos Aires*
H. Fernández
S. Salfate
P. Pino
F. Las Heras
J. Sepúlveda
H. Carvallo
M. Castro
A. Cremaschi
J. Araya (sub. O. Saez)
A. Vera (sub. G. Clavero)
D. Medina
Result 0-1

76: 19th January 1946
v PARAGUAY (SAC) *Buenos Aires*
H. Fernández
S. Salfate (sub. L. Fuenzalida)
A. López
F. Las Heras
J. Sepúlveda
H. Carvallo
M. Castro
A. Cremaschi
J. Araya (sub. L. Mancilla)
A. Vera
D. Medina
Result 2-1 Araya, Mancilla

77: 26th January 1946
v ARGENTINA (SAC)
Buenos Aires
H. Fernández
S. Salfate
A. López
F. Las Heras
J. Sepúlveda
H. Carvallo
M. Castro (sub. J. Alcantara)
A. Cremaschi
L. Mancilla (sub. J. Araya)
A. Vera (sub. J. Penaloza)
D. Medina
Result 1-3 Alcantara

78: 3rd February 1946
v BRAZIL (SAC) *Buenos Aires*
H. Fernández
S. Salfate
A. López
M. Claveria
L. Fuenzalida (sub. F. Las Heras)
H. Carvallo
M. Castro
A. Cremaschi
O. Saez (sub. L. Mancilla)
J. Penaloza (sub. A. Vera)
D. Medina
Result 1-5 Salfate

79: 8th February 1946
v BOLIVIA (SAC) *Buenos Aires*
H. Fernández
S. Salfate
A. López
F. Las Heras
J. Sepúlveda
H. Carvallo
M. Castro (sub. J. Alcantara)
L. Ruiz
J. Araya
A. Cremaschi
D. Medina (sub. D. Romo)
Result 4-1 Araya 3, Cremaschi

80: 6th December 1957
v URUGUAY (SAC) *Guayaquil*
S. Livingstone
F. Urroz
M. Alvarez (sub. J. Negri)
M. Machuca
J. Wood
M. Busquets
F. Riera
A. Prieto (sub. O. Saez)
J. Araya (sub. R. Infante)
J. Penaloza
P.H. López
Result 0-6

81: 9th December 1947
v PERU (SAC) *Guayaquil*
S. Livingstone
R. Baeza
J. Negri
M. Machuca
J. Sepúlveda (sub. D. Acuna)
M. Busquets
F. Riera
C. Varela
O. Saez
J. Penaloza
P.H. López
Result 2-1 Busquets, Varela

82: 11th December 1947
v ECUADOR (SAC) *Guayaquil*
S. Livingstone
F. Urroz
J. Negri
J. Sepúlveda
M. Machuca
M. Busquets (sub. D. Acuna)
A. Balbuena
C. Varela
O. Saez (sub. J. Araya)
J. Penaloza (sub. A. Prieto)
P.H. López
Result 3-0 Penaloza, López 2

83: 16th December 1947
v ARGENTINA (SAC) *Guayaquil*
S. Livingstone
F. Urroz
J. Negri
J. Sepúlveda (sub. D. Acuna)
M. Busquets (sub. F. Campos)
M. Machuca
P.H. López
C. Varela
R. Infante (sub. J. Araya)
J. Penaloza
F. Riera
Result 1-1 Riera

84: 23rd December 1947
v PARAGUAY (SAC) *Guayaquil*
S. Livingstone
R. Baeza
J. Negri
J. Sepúlveda
M. Busquets
M. Machuca
P.H. López
C. Varela
O. Saez
J. Penaloza
F. Riera
Result 0-1

85: 29th December 1947
v COLOMBIA (SAC) *Guayaquil*
S. Livingstone
F. Urroz
J. Negri
J. Sepúlveda
D. Acuna
M. Machuca
F. Riera
P.H. López
C. Varela (sub. J. Penaloza)
J. Araya (sub. R. Infante)
A. Prieto (sub. O. Saez)
Result 4-1 Riera, López, Infante, Saez

86: 31st December 1947
v BOLIVIA (SAC) *Guayaquil*
S. Livingstone
F. Urroz (sub. D. Acuna)
M. Alvarez
M. Machuca
J. Wood
J. Sepúlveda
F. Riera
O. Saez
P.H. López
R. Infante (sub. J. Penaloza)
C. Varela
Result 4-3 Riera, Saez, López, Own Goal

87: 6th April 1949
v BOLIVIA (SAC) *Sao Paulo*
S. Livingstone
M. Flores
F. Urroz
G. Pizarro
M. Busquets
M. Munoz
M. Salamanca (sub. M. Castro)
A. Prieto
C.R. Rojas
A. Cremaschi
F. Riera (sub. P.H. López)
Result 2-3 Salamanca, López

88: 13th April 1949
v BRAZIL (SAC) *Sao Paulo*
S. Livingstone
M. Flores
F. Urroz
M. Machuca
M. Busquets
M. Munoz
F. Riera
A. Prieto
R. Infante (sub. C.R. Rojas)
A. Cremaschi
C. Varela (sub. P.H. López)
Result 1-2 López

89: 17th April 1949
v ECUADOR (SAC) *Rio de Janeiro*
S. Livingstone
M. Flores
F. Urroz
M. Machuca
M. Busquets
M. Munoz
F. Riera
A. Prieto
C.R. Rojas
R. Infante (sub. A. Cremaschi)
C. Varela
Result 1-0 Rojas

90: 20th April 1949
v COLOMBIA (SAC)
Rio de Janeiro
S. Livingstone
M. Flores
F. Urroz
M. Machuca
M. Busquets
M. Munoz
M. Castro
A. Prieto
C.R. Rojas
A. Cremaschi (sub. R. Infante)
C. Varela
Result 1-1 Cremaschi

17

91: 27th April 1949
v PARAGUAY (SAC) *Sao Paulo*
S. Livingstone
M. Flores
F. Urroz
M. Machuca
M. Busquets
E. Hormazábal (sub. M. Munoz)
F. Riera
J. López
A. Cremaschi
C. Varela (sub. R. Infante)
P.H. López
Result 2-4 Riera, Cremaschi

92: 30th April 1949
v PERU (SAC) *Sao Paulo*
S. Livingstone
M. Flores
F. Urroz
M. Machuca
M. Busquets
M. Munoz
M. Castro (sub. P.H. López)
A. Prieto
C.R. Rojas
A. Cremaschi (sub. F. Riera)
C. Varela (sub. R. Infante)
Result 0-3

93: 8th May 1949
v URUGUAY (SAC) *Belo Horizonte*
S. Livingstone
M. Flores
F. Urroz
M. Machuca
M. Busquets
M. Munoz
M. Castro
A. Prieto
C.R. Rojas
A. Cremaschi (sub. R. Infante)
C. Varela
Result 3-1 Rojas, Infante 2

94: 26th February 1950
v BOLIVIA *La Paz*
S. Livingstone
M. Flores
F. Urroz
M. Machuca
C.R. Rojas
E. Hormazábal
F. Riera
A. Prieto
F. Campos
R. Infante
G. Díaz
Result 0-2

95: 12th March 1950
v BOLIVIA *Santiago*
S. Livingstone
M. Machuca
A. Farías
M. Alvarez
M. Busquets
E. Hormazábal
F. Riera
A. Prieto
F. Campos
R. Infante
G. Díaz
Result 5-0 Hormazábal, Prieto, Campos, Díaz 2

96: 7th April 1950
v URUGUAY *Santiago*
R. Quitral
M. Machuca
M. Flores
M. Alvarez
A. Farías
E. Hormazábal
L. Mayanes
F. Campos
C.R. Rojas
A. Cremaschi
G. Díaz
Result 1-5 Díaz

97: 9th April 1950
v URUGUAY *Santiago*
S. Livingstone
A. Farías
F. Roldón
M. Alvarez
M. Busquets
H. Carvallo
L. Mayanes
F. Campos
C.R. Rojas
A. Cremaschi
G. Díaz
Result 2-1 Campos, Díaz

98: 25th June 1950
v ENGLAND (WC) *Rio de Janeiro*
S. Livingstone
A. Farías
F. Roldón
M. Alvarez
M. Busquets
H. Carvallo
L. Mayanes
A. Cremaschi
J. Robledo
M. Munoz
G. Díaz
Result 0-2

99: 29th June 1950
v SPAIN (WC) *Rio de Janeiro*
S. Livingstone
A. Farias
F. Roldón
M. Alvarez
M. Busquets
H. Carvallo
A. Prieto
A. Cremaschi
J. Robledo
M. Munoz
G. Díaz
Result 0-2

100: 2nd July 1950
v UNITED STATES (WC) *Recife*
S. Livingstone
M. Machuca
M. Alvarez
M. Busquets
A. Farías
C.R. Rojas
F. Riera
A. Cremaschi
J. Robledo
A. Prieto
C. Ibanez
Result 5-2 Cremaschi 3, Robledo, Prieto

101: 16th March 1952
v PANAMA (PAC) *Santiago*
H. Fernández
A. Farías
J. Negri
M. Alvarez
R. Cortés
O. Saez
E. Hormazábal
R. Meléndez
M. Munoz
A. Prieto
G. Díaz
Result 6-1 Hormazábal, Meléndez, Munoz, Prieto 3

102: 26th March 1952
v MEXICO (PAC) *Santiago*
H. Fernández
A. Farías
J. Negri
M. Alvarez
R. Cortés
O. Saez (sub. C.R. Rojas)
E. Hormazábal
A. Cremaschi
R. Meléndez
A. Prieto
G. Díaz
Result 4-0 Hormazábal, Prieto, Díaz 2

103: 2nd April 1952
v PERU (PAC) *Santiago*
H. Fernández
A. Farías
J. Negri
M. Alvarez
R. Cortés
O. Saez (sub. C.R. Rojas)
E. Hormazábal (sub. C. Tello)
A. Cremaschi
R. Meléndez
A. Prieto
G. Díaz
Result 3-2 Cremaschi, Meléndez, Prieto

104: 13th April 1952
v URUGUAY (PAC) *Santiago*
S. Livingstone
A. Farías
J. Negri
M. Alvarez
R. Cortés
O. Saez
E. Hormazábal (sub. C. Tello)
A. Cremaschi
R. Meléndez
M. Munoz
G. Díaz
Result 2-0 Cremaschi, Munoz

105: 20th April 1952
v BRAZIL (PAC) *Santiago*
S. Livingstone
A. Farías
J. Negri
M. Alvarez
R. Cortés
O. Saez
E. Hormazábal (sub. C. Tello)
A. Cemaschi
R. Meléndez (sub. C.R. Rojas)
M. Munoz
G. Díaz
Result 0-3

106: 25th February 1953
v PARAGUAY (CA) *Lima*
S. Livingstone
A. Farías
F. Roldón
M. Alvarez
R. Cortés
E. Arenas
E. Hormazábal
A. Cremaschi
R. Meléndez
F. Molina
G. Hurtado
Result 0-3

107: 1st March 1953
v URUGUAY (CA) *Lima*
S. Livingstone
M. Alvarez
F. Roldón
R. Cortés
A. García
O. Saez
E. Hormazábal
A. Cremaschi
R. Meléndez
F. Molina
G. Hurtado
Result 3-2 Molina 3

108: 4th March 1953
v PERU (CA) *Lima*
S. Livingstone
A. Farías
I. Carrasco (sub. F. Roldón)
M. Alvarez
R. Cortés
E. Arenas
E. Hormazábal
A. Cremaschi
R. Meléndez
F. Molina
G. Díaz (sub. C.R. Rojas)
Result 0-0

109: 19th March 1953
v ECUADOR (CA) *Lima*
S. Livingstone
M. Alvarez
F. Roldón
R. Cortés
A. García
O. Saez
E. Hormazábal
A. Cremaschi
C.R. Rojas
F. Molina
G. Díaz
Result 3-0 Molina 2, Díaz

110: 23rd March 1953
v BRAZIL (CA) *Lima*
S. Livingstone
M. Alvarez
F. Roldón
S. Oliver
R. Cortés
A. García
E. Hormazábal
A. Cremaschi
R. Meléndez
F. Molina
O. Saez
Result 2-3 Cremaschi, Molina

111: 28th March 1953
v BOLIVIA (CA) *Lima*
S. Livingstone
A. Farías
I. Carrasco (sub. F. Roldón)
M. Alvarez
R. Cortés
E. Arenas
E. Hormazábal
A. Cremaschi
R. Meléndez (sub. C.R. Rojas)
F. Molina
G. Díaz
Result 2-2 Molina, Díaz

112: 24th May 1953
v ENGLAND *Santiago*
S. Livingstone
A. Farías
G. Nunez
M. Alvarez
C.R. Rojas
R. Cortés
H. Carrasco
A. Cremaschi
R. Meléndez
M. Munoz
G. Díaz
Result 1-2 Díaz

113: 12th July 1953
v SPAIN *Santiago*
S. Livingstone
A. Farías
G. Nunez
M. Alvarez
C.R. Rojas
R. Cortés
E. Hormazábal
A. Cremaschi
J. Robledo
M. Munoz
G. Díaz
Result 1-2 Munoz

114: 26th July 1953
v PERU *Lima*
M. Escuti
A. Farías
F. Roldón
M. Alvarez
C.R. Rojas
R. Cortés
E. Hormazábal
A. Cremaschi
J. Robledo
M. Munoz
G. Díaz (sub. M. Castro)
Result 2-1 Hormazábal, Robledo

115: 28th July 1953
v PERU *Lima*
M. Escuti
A. Farías
F. Roldón
M. Alvarez
C.R. Rojas
R. Cortés
M. Castro
A. Cremaschi
J. Robledo
M. Munoz
G. Díaz
Result 0-5

116: 15th February 1954
v PARAGUAY (WCQ) *Asunción*
S. Livingstone
I. Carrasco (sub. C. Pena)
A. Farías
F. Roldón
R. Cortés
E. Robledo
E. Hormazábal
A. Cremaschi
J. Robledo
M. Munoz
J. Valdes
Result 0-4

117: 21st February 1954
v PARAGUAY (WCQ) *Santiago*
S. Livingstone
C. Pena (sub. I. Carrasco)
A. Farías
F. Roldón
O. Saez
E. Robledo
E. Hormazábal
A. Cremaschi
J. Robledo
M. Munoz
B. Bello
Result 1-3 Robledo

118: 28th February 1954
v BRAZIL (WCQ) *Santiago*
S. Livingstone
M. Alvarez
R. Almeyda
I. Carrasco
R. Cortés
E. Robledo
E. Hormazábal
J. Valdes (sub. C.R. Rojas)
J. Robledo
M. Munoz
R. Meléndez
Result 0-2

119: 14th March 1954
v BRAZIL (WCQ) *Rio de Janeiro*
S. Livingstone
M. Alvarez
R. Almeyda
I. Carrasco
R. Cortés
E. Robledo
E. Hormazábal
C.R. Rojas
J. Robledo
A. Cremaschi (sub. M. Munoz)
R. Meléndez
Result 0-1

120: 17th September 1954
v PERU *Santiago*
M. Escuti
M. Torres
R. Almeyda
I. Carrasco
R. Cortés
C. Pena
B. Musso
J. Valdes
J. Robledo
C. Tello
R. Meléndez
Result 2-1 Musso, Meléndez

22

121: 19th September 1954
v PERU *Santiago*
M. Escuti
M. Torres
R. Almeyda
I. Carrasco
R. Cortés
C. Pena (sub. J. Vera)
B. Musso
R. Meléndez
J. Robledo
C. Tello
G. Díaz
Result 2-4 Meléndez 2

122: 27th February 1955
v ECUADOR (CA) *Santiago*
M. Escuti
R. Almeyda
M. Alvarez
R. Cortés
J. Vera (sub. E. Robledo)
I. Carrasco
E. Hormazábal
R. Meléndez
J. Robledo
S. Espinosa (sub H. Rodríguez)
G. Díaz
Result 7-1 Hormazábal 3, Meléndez,
Robledo, Díaz 2

123: 6th March 1955
v PERU (CA) *Santiago*
M. Escuti
R. Almeyda
M. Alvarez
I. Carrasco
E. Robledo (sub. A. Valjalo)
R. Cortés
E. Hormazábal (sub. J. Ramirez)
M. Munoz
J. Robledo
R. Meléndez
G. Díaz
Result 5-4 Hormazábal, Ramirez, Munoz,
Robledo 2

124: 13th March 1955
v URUGUAY (CA) *Santiago*
M. Escuti
R. Almeyda
M. Alvarez
R. Cortés
I. Carrasco
E. Robledo
G. Díaz
E. Hormazábal
J. Robledo
M. Munoz (sub. R. Meléndez)
J. Ramirez
Result 2-2 Hormazábal, Munoz

125: 20th March 1955
v PARAGUAY (CA) *Santiago*
M. Escuti
R. Almeyda
M. Alvarez
R. Cortés
I. Carrasco
E. Robledo
E. Hormazábal
R. Meléndez
J. Robledo
J. Ramirez (sub. G. Díaz)
M. Munoz
Result 5-0 Hormazábal, Meléndez 2,
Munoz 2

126: 30th March 1955
v ARGENTINA (CA) *Santiago*
M. Escuti
R. Almeyda
I. Carrasco
M. Alvarez
R. Cortés
E. Robledo
E. Hormazábal
R. Meléndez (sub. S. Espinosa)
J. Robledo
M. Munoz (sub. G. Díaz)
J. Ramirez
Result 0-1

127: 18th September 1955
v BRAZIL *Rio de Janeiro*
M. Escuti
R. Almeyda
I. Carrasco
M. Alvarez
R. Cortés
C. Cubillos
E. Hormazábal
R. Meléndez
J. Robledo
M. Munoz
J. Ramirez
Result 1-1 Ramirez

128: 20th September 1955
v BRAZIL *Sao Paulo*
M. Escuti
R. Almeyda
I. Carrasco
M. Alvarez
R. Cortés
C. Cubillos
E. Hormazábal
R. Meléndez
J. Robledo
M. Munoz
J. Ramirez
Result 1-2 Hormazábal

129: 24th January 1956
v BRAZIL (CA) *Montevideo*
M. Escuti
M. Alvarez
I. Carrasco
R. Cortés
R. Almeyda
C. Cubillos
J. Ramirez
E. Hormazábal
R. Meléndez
L. Sánchez
M. Munoz
Result 4-1 Hormazábal 2, Meléndez,
Sánchez

130: 29th January 1956
v ARGENTINA (CA) *Montevideo*
M. Escuti
M. Alvarez
I. Carrasco
R. Cortés
R. Almeyda
C. Cubillos
J. Ramirez
E. Hormazábal
R. Meléndez
M. Munoz
L. Sánchez
Result 0-2

131: 6th February 1956
v URUGUAY (CA) *Montevideo*
M. Escuti
M. Alvarez
I. Carrasco
R. Cortés
R. Almeyda
C. Cubillos
J. Ramirez (sub. J. Fernández)
E. Hormazábal
R. Meléndez
M. Munoz
L. Sánchez
Result 1-2 Ramirez

132: 9th February 1956
v PERU (CA) *Montevideo*
C. Espinosa
M. Alvarez
I. Carrasco
M. Ortiz
R. Almeyda
R. Cortés
J. Ramirez
E. Hormazábal
S. Espinosa (sub. J. Fernández)
M. Munoz
L. Sánchez
Result 4-3 Hormazábal, Fernández, Munoz,
Sánchez

133: 12th February 1956
v PARAGUAY (CA) *Montevideo*
C. Espinosa
M. Alvarez
I. Carrasco
C. Cubillos
R. Almeyda
R. Cortés
J. Ramirez
E. Hormazábal
R. Meléndez
M. Munoz (sub. J. Fernández)
L. Sánchez
Result 2-0 Ramirez, Hormazábal

134: 1st March 1956
v BRAZIL (PAC) *Mexico City*
M. Escuti
M. Alvarez (sub. I. Carrasco)
R. Almeyda
M. Huerta
R. Cortés
C. Cubillos
B. Musso
E. Hormazábal
R. Meléndez
M. Munoz (sub. C. Tello)
L. Sánchez
Result 1-2 Tello

135: 8th March 1956
v COSTA RICA (PAC) *Mexico City*
M. Escuti
M. Alvarez
R. Almeyda
M. Huerta
R. Cortés (sub. I. Carrasco)
C. Cubillos
B. Musso (sub. C. Tello)
E. Hormazábal
R. Meléndez
M. Munoz
L. Sánchez
Result 1-2 Hormazábal

136: 11th March 1956
v ARGENTINA (PAC) *Mexico City*
M. Escuti
M. Alvarez
R. Almeyda
M. Huerta
R. Cortés
C. Cubillos
B. Musso (sub. C. Tello)
E. Hormazábal
R. Meléndez (sub. J. Robledo)
M. Munoz
L. Sánchez
Result 0-3

137: 15th March 1956
v PERU (PAC) *Mexico City*
M. Escuti
I. Carrasco
R. Almeyda
M. Huerta
R. Cortés
C. Cubillos
C. Tello
E. Hormazábal
J. Robledo
M. Munoz (sub. R. Meléndez)
L. Sánchez (sub. G. Díaz)
Result 2-2 Cortés, Díaz

138: 18th March 1956
v MEXICO (PAC) *Mexico City*
M. Escuti
I. Carrasco
R. Almeyda
M. Huerta
R. Cortés
C. Cubillos
C. Tello
E. Hormazábal
J. Robledo (sub. R. Meléndez)
M. Munoz
G. Díaz
Result 1-2 Tello

139: 26th August 1956
v CZECHOSLOVAKIA *Santiago*
M. Escuti
I. Carrasco
R. Almeyda
M. Ortiz
R. Cortés
C. Cubillos
J. Ramirez
E. Hormazábal
J. Robledo
C. Tello (sub. J. Fernández)
G. Díaz (sub. L. Sánchez)
Result 3-0 Hormazábal, Robledo 2

140: 13th March 1957
v BRAZIL (CA) *Lima*
M. Escuti
M. Torres
M. Ortiz
C. Pena
R. Cortés (sub. G. Carrasco)
I. Carrasco
J. Ramirez
T. Pico
S. Espinosa
C. Tello (sub. J. Fernández)
L. Sánchez
Result 2-4 Ramirez, Fernández

141: 16th March 1957
v PERU (CA) *Lima*
M. Escuti
M. Torres
C. Cubillos
C. Pena
G. Carrasco
I. Carrasco
J. Ramirez
A. Prieto (sub. T. Pico)
J. Robledo
J. Fernández
L. Sánchez (sub. R. Aguila)
Result 0-1

142: 21st March 1957
v COLOMBIA (CA) *Lima*
M. Escuti
M. Torres (sub. R. Almeyda)
C. Cubillos
C. Pena
G. Carrasco
S. Valdes
J. Ramirez
S. Espinosa
C. Verdejo
C. Tello
R. Aguila
Result 3-2 Espinosa, Verdejo 2

143: 24th March 1957
v ECUADOR (CA) *Lima*
M. Escuti
R. Almeyda
C. Cubillos
C. Pena
G. Carrasco
S. Valdes
J. Ramirez (sub. L. Sánchez)
T. Pico (sub. A. Prieto)
C. Verdejo
C. Tello
R. Aguila
Result 2-2 Ramirez 2

144: 28th March 1957
v ARGENTINA (CA) *Lima*
M. Escuti
C. Cubillos
R. Almeyda
C. Pena
M. Ortiz
A. Morales
J. Ramirez (sub. L. Sánchez)
T. Pico
J. Robledo
J. Fernández
R. Aguila (sub. C. Tello)
Result 2-6 Fernández 2

145: 1st April 1957
v URUGUAY (CA) *Lima*
F. Nietsche
C. Pena
R. Almeyda
S. Valdes
M. Ortiz
A. Morales
R. Aguila
T. Pico
J. Robledo
J. Fernández
J. Ramirez
Result 0-2

146: 15th September 1957
v BRAZIL *Santiago*
R. Quitral
C. Pena
J. Vera
R. Salazar
M. Ortiz
A. Morales
V. Astorga
J. Ramirez
J. Robledo (sub. R. Meléndez)
J. Fernández
G. Díaz
Result 1-0 Meléndez

147: 18th September 1957
v BRAZIL *Santiago*
R. Quitral
C. Pena
J. Vera
R. Salazar
A. Morales
E. Hormazábal
V. Astorga
J. Ramirez
R. Meléndez (sub. J. Robledo)
J. Fernández
G. Díaz
Result 1-1 Fernández

148: 22nd September 1957
v BOLIVIA (WCQ) *Santiago*
R. Quitral
C. Pena
J. Vera
R. Salazar
A. Morales
E. Hormazábal
V. Astorga
J. Ramirez
J. Robledo
J. Fernández
G. Díaz
Result 2-1 Hormazábal, Ramirez

149: 29th September 1957
v BOLIVIA (WCQ) *La Paz*
R. Quitral
C. Pena
J. Vera
M. Torres
J. Toro
Os. Díaz
M. Ortiz
R. Aguila
J. Robledo
J. Ramirez
L. Sánchez
Result 0-3

150: 13th October 1957
v ARGENTINA (WCQ) *Santiago*
R. Quitral
C. Pena
Ju. Toro
J. Vera
M. Torres
Ju. Rojas
J. Ramirez
J. Robledo
R. Meléndez
J. Fernández
G. Díaz
Result 0-2

151: 20th October 1957
v ARGENTINA (WCQ)
Buenos Aires
R. Quitral
S. Navarro
V. Astorga
J. Vera
R. Salazar
Ju. Rojas
H. Carrasco
E. Hormazábal
Juan Soto
J. Ramirez
L. Sánchez
Result 0-4

152: 7th March 1959
v ARGENTINA (CA) *Buenos Aires*
R. Caloma
S. Valdes
M. Torres (sub. R. Sánchez)
S. Navarro
J. Vera
H. Rodríguez
Juan Soto
L.H. Alvarez
A. Tobar (sub. E. Rojas)
L. Sánchez
Jo. Toro
Result 1-6 Alvarez

153: 11th March 1959
v PARAGUAY (CA) *Buenos Aires*
R. Caloma
S. Valdes
R. Sánchez
S. Navarro
J. Vera
H. Rodríguez
M. Soto
L.H. Alvarez
Juan Soto (sub. E. Rojas)
L. Sánchez
Jo. Toro
Result 1-2 L. Sánchez

154: 15th March 1959
v BRAZIL (CA) *Buenos Aires*
R. Caloma
S. Valdes
R. Sánchez
S. Navarro
J. Vera
H. Rodríguez
M. Moreno
L.H. Alvarez (sub. E. Rojas)
Juan Soto (sub. C. Verdejo)
L. Sánchez
M. Soto
Result 0-3

155: 21st March 1959
v PERU (CA) *Buenos Aires*
R. Caloma
S. Valdes
R. Sánchez
S. Navarro
J. Vera
H. Rodríguez
M. Moreno
Jo. Toto (sub. R. Hoffman)
Juan Soto
L. Sánchez (sub. A. Tobar)
M. Soto
Result 1-1 Moreno

156: 26th March 1959
v BOLIVIA (CA) *Buenos Aires*
R. Caloma
S. Valdes
R. Sánchez
S. Navarro (sub. L. Eyzaguirre)
J. Vera (sub. Ju. Rojas)
H. Rodríguez
M. Moreno (sub. E. Rojas)
M. Soto
Juan Soto
L. Sánchez
R. Hoffman
*Result 5-2 M. Soto 2, Juan Soto 2,
L. Sánchez*

157: 2nd April 1959
v URUGUAY (CA) *Buenos Aires*
R. Caloma
R. Sánchez
H. Rodríguez
S. Valdes
J. Vera (sub. Ju. Rojas)
S. Navarro
M. Moreno
Manuel Soto
Juan Soto
L. Sánchez (sub. E. Rojas)
R. Hoffman (sub. A. Tobar)
Result 1-0 Moreno

158: 18th November 1959
v ARGENTINA *Santiago*
R. Caloma
L. Eyzaguirre
R. Sánchez
S. Navarro
J. Luco (sub. C. Contreras)
H. Rodríguez
M. Moreno
A. Tobar (sub. J. Ríos)
R. Meléndez (sub. Juan Soto)
L. Sánchez
B. Bello
Result 4-2 Ríos, L. Sánchez, Bello 2

159: 16th March 1960
v FRANCE *Paris*
R. Caloma
L. Eyzaguirre
R. Sánchez
S. Navarro (sub. I. Carrasco)
J. Luco
H. Rodríguez
L. Sánchez
M. Moreno
J. Soto
A. Tobar
B. Bello
Result 0-6

160: 23rd March 1960
v WEST GERMANY *Stuttgart*
R. Caloma
L. Eyzaguirre
R. Sánchez
S. Navarro
J. Luco
H. Rodríguez
M. Moreno
A. Tobar (sub. A. Fouilloux)
Juan Soto
L. Sánchez
B. Bello
Result 1-2 Soto

161: 30 March 1960
v EIRE *Dublin*
R. Caloma
L. Eyzaguirre
R. Sánchez
S. Navarro
J. Luco
H. Rodríguez
M. Moreno
A. Fouilloux
J. Soto
L. Sánchez
B. Musso
Result 0-2

162: 6th April 1960
v SWITZERLAND *Basle*
R. Caloma
L. Eyzaguirre
R. Sánchez
S. Navarro
J. Luco
H. Rodríguez
M. Moreno
A. Fouilloux (sub. A. Tobar)
Juan Soto
L. Sánchez
B. Bello
Result 2-4 Tobar, Soto

163: 13th April 1960
v BELGIUM *Brussels*
R. Caloma
L. Eyzaguirre
R. Sánchez
S. Navarro
J. Luco
H. Rodríguez
M. Moreno
B. Musso
Juan Soto
A. Tobar
L. Sánchez (sub. B. Bello)
Result 1-1 Musso

164: 1st June 1960
v URUGUAY *Santiago*
M. Escuti
L. Eyzaguirre
S. Valdes
S. Navarro
J. Luco
H. Rodríguez
M. Moreno
B. Musso
J. Ramirez
A. Fouilloux (sub. A. Tobar)
L. Sánchez
Result 2-3 Moreno, Fouilloux

165: 5th June 1960
v URUGUAY *Montevideo*
M. Escuti
L. Eyzaguirre
S. Valdes
S. Navarro
J. Luco
H. Rodríguez
M. Moreno
B. Musso
J. Ramirez
A. Fouilloux (sub. B. Bello)
L. Sánchez
Result 2-2 Sánchez 2

166: 29th June 1960
v BRAZIL *Rio de Janeiro*
M. Escuti
L. Eyzaguirre (sub. R. Sánchez)
S. Valdez
C. Contreras
J. Luco (sub. R. Cortés)
H. Rodríguez
M. Moreno
B. Musso
J. Ramirez
A. Tobar (sub. A. Fouilloux)
L. Sánchez
Result 0-4

167: 14th July 1960
v SPAIN *Santiago*
M. Escuti
L. Eyzaguirre (sub. S. Navarro)
S. Valdes
R. Cortés
F. Navarro
H. Rodríguez
M. Moreno
B. Musso
J. Ramirez
A. Fouilloux
L. Sánchez
Result 0-4

168: 17th July 1960
v SPAIN *Santiago*
M. Escuti
S. Navarro
S. Valdes
R. Cortés
F. Navarro
H. Rodríguez
M. Moreno
B. Musso
J. Ramirez
Jo. Toro
L. Sánchez
Result 1-4 Musso

169: 18th December 1960
v PARAGUAY *Santiago*
M. Escuti
L. Eyzaguirre
S. Navarro
C. Contreras
F. Navarro
H. Rodríguez
M. Moreno
J. Ramirez
R. Cabrera
Jo. Toro
L. Sánchez
Result 4-1 Moreno 2, Cabrera, Sánchez

170: 21st December 1960
v PARAGUAY *Valparaíso*
M. Escuti
L. Eyzaguirre
S. Navarro
C. Contreras
F. Navarro
H. Rodríguez (sub. M. Ortiz)
M. Moreno
J. Ramirez (sub. A. Fouilloux)
R. Cabrera
Jo. Toro
L. Sánchez
Result 3-1 Moreno, Cabrera 2

171: 19th March 1961
v PERU *Santiago*
M. Astorga
L. Eyzaguirre
S. Navarro
C. Contreras
F. Navarro
M. Ortiz
M. Moreno (sub. R. Betta)
J. Ramirez
Juan Soto
Jo. Toro
L. Sánchez
Result 5-2 Betta, Soto, Toro, Sánchez

172: 26th March 1961
v WEST GERMANY *Santiago*
M. Escuti
L. Eyzaguirre
S. Navarro
C. Contreras
R. Sánchez
E. Rojas
R. Betta
Jo. Toro
Juan Soto
L. Sánchez
J. Ramirez
Result 3-1 Rojas, R. Sánchez

173: 7th May 1961
v BRAZIL *Santiago*
M. Escuti
L. Eyzaguirre
S. Navarro
C. Contreras
R. Sánchez
E. Rojas
A. Fouilloux
Jo. Toro
Juan Soto
L. Sánchez
R. Hoffman
Result 1-2 Soto

174: 11th May 1961
v BRAZIL *Santiago*
M. Escuti
L. Eyzaguirre
S. Navarro
C. Contreras
R. Sánchez
E. Rojas
R. Betta (sub. J. Ramirez)
Jo. Toro
A. Tobar
L. Sánchez (sub. Juan Soto)
R. Hoffman (sub. B. Musso)
Result 0-1

175: 12th October 1961
v URUGUAY *Santiago*
M. Escuti
L. Eyzaguirre
S. Navarro
C. Contreras
R. Sánchez
E. Rojas
M. Moreno
A. Fouilloux
A. Tobar
J. Ramirez
L. Sánchez
Result 2-3 Moreno, Fouilloux

176: 22nd November 1961
v U.S.S.R. *Santiago*
M. Escuti
L. Eyzaguirre
S. Navarro
C. Contreras
R. Sánchez
E. Rojas
M. Moreno
Jo. Toro
H. Landa
L. Sánchez
J. Ramirez
Result 0-1

177: 9th December 1961
v HUNGARY *Santiago*
M. Escuti
S. Valdes
H. Lepe
H. Rodríguez
H. Cruz
A. Sepúlveda
M. Moreno
Jo. Toro
H. Landa
A. Fouilloux
L. Sánchez
Result 5-1 Sepúlveda, Landa, Fouilloux, Sánchez 2

178: 13th December 1961
v HUNGARY *Santiago*
M. Escuti
S. Valdes
H. Lepe
H. Rodríguez
H. Cruz
A. Sepúlveda
M. Moreno
Jo. Toro
H. Landa
A. Fouilloux
L. Sánchez
Result 0-0

179: 30th May 1962
v SWITZERLAND (WC) *Santiago*
M. Escuti
L. Eyzaguirre
R. Sánchez
S. Navarro
C. Contreras
E. Rojas
J. Ramirez
Jo. Toro
H. Landa
A. Fouilloux
L. Sánchez
Result 3-1 Ramirez, L. Sánchez 2

180: 2nd June 1962
v ITALY (WC) *Santiago*
M. Escuti
L. Eyzaguirre
R. Sánchez
S. Navarro
C. Contreras
E. Rojas
J. Ramirez
Jo. Toro
H. Landa
A. Fouilloux
L. Sánchez
Result 2-0 Ramirez, Toro

181: 6th June 1962
v WEST GERMANY (WC)
Santiago
M. Escuti
L. Eyzaguirre
S. Navarro
C. Contreras
R. Sánchez
E. Rojas
M. Moreno
A. Tobar
H. Landa
L. Sánchez
J. Ramirez
Result 0-2

182: 10th June 1962
v U.S.S.R. (WC) *Arica*
M. Escuti
L. Eyzaguirre
S. Navarro
C. Contreras
R. Sánchez
E. Rojas
J. Ramirez
Jo. Toro
H. Landa
A. Tobar
L. Sánchez
Result 2-1

183: 13th June 1962
v BRAZIL (WC) *Santiago*
M. Escuti
L. Eyzaguirre
H. Rodríguez
C. Contreras
R. Sánchez
E. Rojas
J. Ramirez
Jo. Toro
H. Landa
A. Tobar
L. Sánchez
Result 2-4 Toro, L. Sánchez

184: 16th June 1962
v YUGOSLAVIA (WC) *Santiago*
A. Godoy
L. Eyzaguirre
H. Rodríguez
H. Cruz
R. Sánchez
E. Rojas
J. Ramirez
Jo. Toro
C. Campos
A. Tobar
L. Sánchez
Result 1-0 Rojas

185: 7th November 1962
v ARGENTINA *Santiago*
M. Escuti (sub. A. Godoy)
R. Sánchez
H. Rodríguez
L. Eyzaguirre
C. Contreras
E. Rojas
O. Ramirez
A. Fouilloux (sub. E. Hormazábal)
H. Landa (sub. C. Verdejo)
C. Ibanez
F. Valdez
Result 1-1 Landa

186: 21st November 1962
v ARGENTINA *Buenos Aires*
M. Escuti
R. Sánchez
S. Navarro
A. Valentini
C. Contreras
E. Rojas
O. Ramirez (sub. E. Hormazábal)
A. Fouilloux
H. Landa (sub. R. Cabrera)
F. Valdez (sub. C. Verdejo)
L. Sánchez
Result 0-1

187: 23rd March 1963
v URUGUAY *Montevideo*
M. Escuti
L. Eyzaguirre
R. Sánchez
A. Valentini
C. Contreras
M. Ortiz
J. Ramirez
A. Fouilloux (sub. E. Hormazábal)
H. Landa
R. Marcos (sub. B. Bello)
L. Sánchez
Result 2-3 Ramirez 2

188: 24th July 1963
v URUGUAY *Santiago*
M. Astorga
L. Eyzaguirre
R. Sánchez
A. Valentini
C. Contreras
M. Ortiz
J. Ramirez
A. Fouilloux (sub. E. Hormazábal)
A. Tobar
R. Marcos (sub. B. Bello)
L. Sánchez
Result 0-0

189: 24th September 1964
v ARGENTINA *Buenos Aires*
M. Astorga
L. Eyzaguirre
R. Sánchez
H. Villanueva
C. Contreras (sub. H. Cruz)
O. Aravena (sub. A. Sepúlveda)
M. Moreno (sub. E. Méndez)
A. Fouilloux
A. Tobar
R. Marcos
L. Sánchez
Result 0-5

190: 14th October 1964
v ARGENTINA *Santiago*
A. Godoy
L. Eyzaguirre
R. Sánchez
A. Valentini
C. Contreras
O. Aravena (sub. G. Ross)
P. Araya
C. Verdejo
H. Landa
R. Marcos (sub. G. Yávar)
L. Sánchez (sub. O. Ramirez)
Result 1-1 Verdejo

191: 15th April 1965
v PERU *Santiago*
A. Godoy
A. Valentini
H. Donoso
H. Villanueva
C. Contreras
R. Hodge
P. Araya
R. Marcos
H. Landa
A. Fouilloux (sub. O. Ramirez)
L. Sánchez
Result 4-1 Araya 2, Landa 2

192: 28th April 1965
v PERU *Santiago*
A. Godoy
A. Valentini
H. Donoso
H. Villanueva
C. Contreras
R. Hodge
P. Araya
R. Marcos
H. Landa
A. Fouilloux (sub. O. Ramirez)
L. Sánchez
Result 1-0 Araya

193: 9th May 1965
v URUGUAY *Santiago*
A. Godoy
A. Valentini
H. Donoso
H. Villanueva
C. Contreras
R. Hodge
P. Araya
I. Prieto
R. Cabrera
A. Fouilloux (sub. R. Marcos)
L. Sánchez
Result 0-0

194: 16th May 1965
v URUGUAY *Montevideo*
J. Olivares
A. Valentini
H. Donoso (sub. E. Figueroa)
H. Villanueva
C. Contreras
R. Hodge
P. Araya
I. Prieto
R. Cabrera (sub. J. Ramirez)
A. Fouilloux
L. Sánchez
Result 1-1 Sánchez

195: 14th July 1965
v ARGENTINA *Buenos Aires*
F. Nietsche
A. Valentini
H. Donoso
H. Villanueva (sub. O. Ramirez)
C. Contreras
R. Hodge
P. Araya
I. Prieto
R. Cabrera (sub. C. Campos)
A. Fouilloux (sub. R. Marcos)
L. Sánchez
Result 0-1

196: 21st July 1965
v ARGENTINA *Santiago*
F. Nietsche (sub. M. Astorga)
A. Valentini
H. Donoso
J. González
C. Contreras
R. Hodge
P. Araya
I. Prieto
C. Campos (sub. H. Landa)
A. Fouilloux (sub. O. Ramirez)
L. Sánchez
Result 1-1 Sánchez

197: 1st August 1965
v COLOMBIA (WCQ) *Santiago*
F. Nietsche
A. Valentini
H. Donoso
J. González
C. Contreras
R. Hodge
E. Méndez
I. Prieto
C. Campos
A. Fouilloux
L. Sánchez
Result 7-2 Méndez 2, Prieto, Campos,
Fouilloux 2, Sánchez

198: 7th August 1965
v COLOMBIA (WCQ) *Barranquilla*
F. Nietsche
A. Valentini
H. Donoso
J. González
C. Contreras
R. Hodge
E. Méndez
I. Prieto
H. Landa
A. Fouilloux
L. Sánchez
Result 0-2

199: 15th August 1965
v ECUADOR (WCQ) *Guayaquil*
M. Astorga
A. Valentini
H. Donoso
J. González
C. Contreras
O. Aravena
R. Marcos
I. Prieto
C. Campos
A. Fouilloux
L. Sánchez
Result 2-2 Prieto, Campos

200: 22nd August 1965
v ECUADOR (WCQ) *Santiago*
M. Astorga
A. Valentini
H. Donoso
J. González
C. Contreras
R. Hodge
R. Marcos
I. Prieto
R. Cabrera
A. Fouilloux
L. Sánchez
Result 3-1 Marcos, Fouilloux, Sánchez

201: 12th October 1965
v ECUADOR (WCQ) *Lima*
A. Godoy
L. Eyzaguirre
H. Donoso
J. González
H. Cruz
I. Prieto
P. Araya
R. Marcos
C. Campos
A. Fouilloux
L. Sánchez
Result 2-1 Marcos, Sánchez

202: 23rd February 1966
v U.S.S.R. *Santiago*
A. Godoy
L. Eyzaguirre
H. Donoso
H. Villanueva
H. Cruz
E. Rojas
P. Araya
R. Marcos
C. Campos (sub. J. Gallardo)
A. Fouilloux (sub. A. Tobar)
L. Sánchez
Result 0-2

203: 17th April 1966
v BRAZIL *Santiago*
A. Godoy
L. Eyzaguirre
H. Donoso
H. Villanueva
H. Cruz
R. Hodge
R. Marcos
P. Araya
C. Campos (sub. J. Gallardo)
A. Fouilloux
L. Sánchez (sub. L. Véliz)
Result 0-1

204: 20th April 1966
v BRAZIL *Vina del Mar*
A. Godoy
L. Eyzaguirre
H. Donoso
H. Villanueva (sub. C. Contreras)
H. Cruz
I. Prieto
R. Marcos
P. Araya
A. Tobar
F. Valdes
L. Sánchez (sub. J. Ramirez)
Result 2-1 Araya, Valdes

205: 11th May 1966
v MEXICO *Mexico City*
A. Godoy
L. Eyzaguirre
H. Cruz
E. Figueroa
H. Villanueva
R. Marcos
P. Araya
F. Valdes
H. Landa
G. Yávar
L. Sánchez
Result 0-1

206: 15th May 1966
v BRAZIL *Sao Paulo*
A. Godoy
L. Eyzaguirre
H. Cruz
E. Figueroa
H. Villanueva
R. Marcos
P. Araya
G. Yávar
H. Landa
A. Fouilloux
L. Sánchez (sub. J. Ramirez)
Result 1-1 Yávar

207: 19th May 1966
v BRAZIL *Rio de Janeiro*
A. Godoy
L. Eyzaguirre
E. Figueroa
H. Villanueva
H. Cruz
R. Marcos
P. Araya
G. Yávar
H. Landa (sub. A. Tobar)
A. Fouilloux (sub. J. Ramirez)
L. Sánchez
Result 0-1

208: 22nd May 1966
v WALES *Santiago*
A. Godoy
L. Eyzaguirre
E. Figueroa
H. Villanueva
H. Cruz
R. Marcos
P. Araya
G. Yávar (sub. F. Valdes)
A. Tobar
A. Fouilloux (sub. J. Ramirez)
L. Sánchez
Result 2-0 Marcos, Tobar

209: 29th May 1966
v MEXICO *Santiago*
A. Godoy
L. Eyzaguirre
E. Figueroa
H. Villanueva
H. Cruz
R. Marcos
P. Araya
I. Prieto
A. Tobar
A. Fouilloux
L. Sánchez
Result 0-1

210: 2nd July 1966
v EAST GERMANY *Leipzig*
A. Godoy
L. Eyzaguirre
H. Cruz
E. Figueroa
H. Villanueva
I. Prieto
R. Marcos
P. Araya
A. Tobar
A. Fouilloux
L. Sánchez
Result 2-5 Tobar, Fouilloux

211: 13th July 1966
v ITALY (WC) *Sunderland*
J. Olivares
L. Eyzaguirre
H. Cruz
E. Figueroa
H. Villanueva
I. Prieto
R. Marcos
P. Araya
A. Tobar
A. Fouilloux
L. Sánchez
Result 0-2

212: 15th July 1966
v NORTH KOREA (WC)
Middlesbrough
J. Olivares
A. Valentini
H. Cruz
E. Figueroa
H. Villanueva
I. Prieto
R. Marcos
A. Fouilloux
H. Landa
P. Araya
L. Sánchez
Result 1-1 Marcos

213: 20th July 1966
v U.S.S.R. (WC) *Sunderland*
J. Olivares
A. Valentini
H. Cruz
E. Figueroa
H. Villanueva
R. Marcos
I. Prieto
P. Araya
H. Landa
G. Yávar
L. Sánchez
Result 1-2 Marcos

214: 30th November 1966
v COLOMBIA (CA) *Santiago*
J. Olivares
A. Valentini
H. Cruz
E. Figueroa
H. Villanueva
R. Hodge
I. Prieto
P. Araya
C. Campos
R. Marcos
M. Saavedra (sub. O. Castro)
Result 5-2 Prieto, Araya, Saavedra, Castro 2

215: 11th December 1966
v COLOMBIA (CA) *Bogota*
J. Olivares
A. Valentini
E. Figueroa
H. Villanueva
H. Cruz
R. Hodge
I. Prieto
P. Araya
C. Campos
R. Marcos (sub. A. Tobar)
O. Castro
Result 0-0

216: 18th January 1967
v VENEZUELA (CA) *Montevideo*
J. Olivares
J. Adriazola
H. Cruz
E. Figueroa
H. Villanueva
R. Hodge
I. Prieto
P. Araya
C. Campos (sub. J. Gallardo)
R. Marcos
M. Saavedra (sub. O. Castro)
Result 2-0 Marcos 2

217: 22nd January 1967
v PARAGUAY (CA) *Montevideo*
J. Olivares
J. Adriazola
H. Cruz
E. Figueroa
H. Villanueva
R. Hodge
P. Araya
I. Prieto
J. Gallardo
R. Marcos
O. Castro
Result 4-2 Araya, Gallardo 3

218: 26th January 1967
v URUGUAY (CA) *Montevideo*
J. Olivares
J. Adriazola
H. Cruz
E. Figueroa
E. Herrera
R. Hodge
P. Araya
I. Prieto
J. Gallardo
R. Marcos (sub. A. Tobar)
O. Castro
Result 2-2 Gallardo, Marcos

219: 28th January 1967
v ARGENTINA (CA) *Montevideo*
J. Olivares
J. Adriazola
E. Herrera
E. Figueroa
H. Cruz
R. Hodge (sub. F. Moris)
P. Araya
I. Prieto
J. Gallardo
R. Marcos
O. Castro
Result 0-2

220: 1st February 1967
v BOLIVIA (CA) *Montevideo*
J. Olivares
J. Adriazola (sub. H. Castaneda)
H. Cruz
E. Figueroa
E. Herrera
R. Hodge (sub. A. Tobar)
P. Araya
I. Prieto
J. Gallardo
R. Marcos
O. Castro
Result 0-0

221: 15th August 1967
v ARGENTINA *Santiago*
J. Olivares
H. Berly
A. Quintano
H. Cruz
E. Herrera
C. Horsch
P. Araya
I. Prieto
C. Reinoso
L. Sánchez
A. Fouilloux
Result 1-0 Araya

222: 19th September 1967
v BRAZIL *Santiago*
J. Olivares
H. Berly
A. Quintano
H. Cruz
E. Herrera
R. Marcos
P. Araya
I. Prieto
C. Reinoso (sub. J. Gallardo)
L. Sánchez
A. Fouilloux
Result 0-1

223: 18th November 1967
v ARGENTINA *Santiago*
J. Olivares
H. Berly
H. Cruz
A. Quintano
E. Herrera
R. Marcos
P. Araya
I. Prieto
C. Reinoso
A. Fouilloux
L. Sánchez
Result 3-1 Reinoso, Fouilloux 2

224: 17th December 1967
v U.S.S.R. *Santiago*
J. Olivares
H. Berly
H. Cruz
A. Quintano
E. Herrera
R. Hodge
P. Araya
A. Fouilloux
C. Reinoso
R. Marcos (sub. I. Prieto)
O. Castro
Result 1-4 Reinoso

225: 18th August 1968
v PERU *Lima*
J. Olivares
H. Berly
H. Cruz
R. Angulo
E. Herrera
C. Reinoso
F. Valdes
A. Fouilloux
O. Ramirez
R. Marcos
O. Castro (sub. L. Sánchez)
Result 1-2 Valdes

226: 21st August 1968
v PERU *Lima*
J. Olivares
H. Berly
H. Cruz
R. Angulo
E. Herrera
C. Reinoso
F. Valdes
A. Fouilloux
O. Ramirez
R. Marcos
L. Sánchez
Result 0-0

227: 28th August 1968
v MEXICO *Mexico City*
J. Olivares
H. Berly
H. Cruz
A. Quintano
E. Herrera
C. Reinoso
F. Valdes
A. Fouilloux
O. Ramirez
A. Olivares
L. Sánchez
Result 1-3 Sánchez

228: 23rd October 1968
v MEXICO *Santiago*
J. Olivares
H. Berly
H. Cruz
R. Angulo
E. Herrera
C. Reinoso (sub. A. Arias)
A. Lara
A. Fouilloux (sub. P. Araya)
O. Ramirez
F. Valdes
L. Sánchez (sub. A. Olivares)
Result 3-1 Araya, Olivares 2

229: 27th November 1968
v ARGENTINA *Rosario*
J. Olivares
H. Berly
H. Cruz
R. Angulo
J. Rodríguez
C. Reinoso
A. Lara
A. Fouilloux
O. Ramirez
F. Valdes (sub. E. Cuevas)
O. Castro (sub. A. Olivares)
Result 0-4

230: 4th December 1968
v ARGENTINA *Santiago*
J. Olivares (sub. L. Vallejos)
H. Berly (sub. J. Gallardo)
H. Cruz
R. Angulo
E. Herrera
C. Reinoso
A. Lara
F. Valdes
P. Araya
A. Fouilloux
O. Castro (sub. A. Olivares)
Result 2-1 Fouilloux, Olivares

231: 18th December 1968
v WEST GERMANY *Santiago*
L. Vallejos
H. Berly
H. Cruz
R. Angulo
E. Herrera
C. Reinoso
A. Lara
F. Valdes
P. Araya
A. Fouilloux
O. Castro (sub. A. Olivares)
Result 2-1 Araya, Fouilloux

232: 28th May 1969
v ARGENTINA *Santiago*
A. Nef
J. Rodríguez
G. Laube
A. Quintano
D. Díaz
R. Hodge
F. Valdes (sub. A. Lara)
A. Fouilloux
A. Olivares
G. Yávar (sub. C. Reinoso)
L. Véliz
Result 1-1 Véliz

233: 8th June 1969
v PARAGUAY *Asunción*
A. Nef
J. Rodríguez (sub. J. Gallardo)
G. Laube
A. Quintano
D. Díaz
R. Hodge
F. Valdes
A. Fouilloux
A. Olivares (sub. P. Araya)
G. Yávar (sub. C. Reinoso)
L. Véliz
Result 0-1

234: 11th June 1969
v ARGENTINA *La Plata*
A. Nef
J. Rodríguez
G. Laube
A. Quintano
D. Díaz
R. Hodge
F. Valdes
A. Fouilloux
A. Olivares
G. Yávar (sub. C. Reinoso)
L. Véliz (sub. A. Lara)
Result 1-2 Olivares

235: 15th June 1969
v COLOMBIA *Bogota*
A. Nef
J. Rodríguez
G. Laube
A. Quintano
D. Díaz
R. Hodge
F. Valdes
C. Reinoso
P. Araya
A. Olivares
A. Fouilloux
Result 3-3 Laube, Reinoso, Fouilloux

236: 22nd June 1969
v EAST GERMANY *Magdeburg*
A. Nef
J. Rodríguez
G. Laube
A. Quintano
D. Díaz
R. Hodge
F. Valdes
C. Reinoso
P. Araya
A. Olivares (sub. G. Yávar)
A. Fouilloux
Result 1-0 Yávar

237: 6th July 1969
v PARAGUAY *Santiago*
A. Nef
J. Rodríguez
G. Laube
A. Quintano
D. Díaz
R. Hodge
F. Valdes
C. Reinoso
P. Araya
A. Olivares (sub. R. Marcos)
A. Fouilloux (sub. C. Caszely)
Result 0-0

238: 13th July 1969
v URUGUAY (WCQ) *Santiago*
A. Nef
J. Rodríguez
G. Laube
A. Quintano
D. Díaz
R. Hodge
F. Valdes
C. Reinoso
P. Araya
A. Olivares
A. Fouilloux (sub. G. Yávar)
Result 0-0

239: 27th July 1969
v ECUADOR (WCQ) *Santiago*
A. Nef
J. Rodríguez
G. Laube
A. Quintano
D. Díaz
R. Hodge
F. Valdes
C. Reinoso
P. Araya
A. Olivares (sub. R. Marcos)
L. Véliz
Result 4-1 Valdes 2, Olivares 2

240: 3rd August 1969
v ECUADOR (WCQ) *Guayaquil*
A. Nef
J. Rodríguez
G. Laube
A. Quintano
D. Díaz
R. Hodge
C. Reinoso
P. Araya (sub. R. Hoffman)
A. Olivares
R. Marcos (sub. G. Yávar)
L. Véliz
Result 1-1 Olivares

241: 10th August 1969
v URUGUAY (WCQ) *Montevideo*
A. Nef
J. Rodríguez
G. Laube
A. Quintano
D. Díaz
R. Hodge
C. Reinoso
R. Hoffman
A. Olivares
G. Yávar
L. Véliz (sub. A. Lara)
Result 0-2

242: 22nd March 1970
v BRAZIL *Sao Paulo*
M. Astorga
J. Rodríguez
H. Cruz (sub. A. Arias)
A. Quintano
D. Díaz
R. Hodge
F. Valdes
R. Hoffman
P. Araya
O. Castro (sub. A. Fouilloux)
L. Véliz
Result 0-5

243: 26th March 1970
v BRAZIL *Rio de Janeiro*
M. Astorga
J. Rodríguez
E. Herrera
A. Quintano
D. Díaz
R. Hodge
F. Valdes
O. Castro
P. Araya
A. Fouilloux (sub. G. Yávar)
L. Véliz
Result 1-2 Castro

244: 4th October 1970
v BRAZIL *Santiago*
M. Astorga
J. Rodríguez
A. Arias (sub. E. Herrera)
A. Quintano
D. Díaz
R. Hodge
F. Valdes
O. Castro
S. Messen
A. Fouilloux
L. Véliz (sub. P. Araya)
Result 1-5 Messen